A.S.K.

Ask. Seek. Knock.

Audrey Black

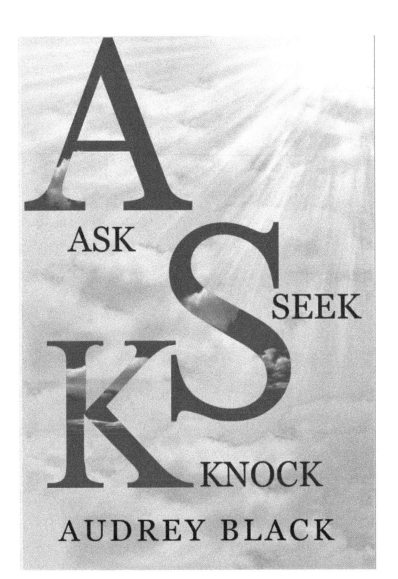

ASK

SEEK

KNOCK

AUDREY BLACK

Audrey Black

ISBN: 9798685547057

Unless otherwise indicated, scripture quotations are
King James Version from the Holy Bible.
All definitions are from New Oxford American Dictionary.

DEDICATION

This book is dedicated to the Lord, my Provider, who brings illumination to all things.

Thank you for clarity on all You direct us to do.

These are Your words to Your people. Therefore, all glory goes to You. You cause hope to be true and dreams to come to pass through the desires You give us, and for that, Sir, I am grateful!

CONTENTS

INTRODUCTION

HOW THIS INFORMATION CAME TO ME WAS nothing less than a miracle. I was sitting in my room one day, working on a crossword puzzle on my phone, when God led me to text a friend. He wanted to use me to answer some questions she asked Him. Discerning their conversation, confirmation came when I heard God say, *"Tell her I said all she needs to do is ask, and I will grant her request."* After I texted her the message, He said to me, *"Now she's going to say to herself, but I already asked! Tell her I said, no she did not."* Bananas, right?

Keep in mind, my friend is an educator. Her response echoed the Lord's voice. "I thought I already asked. Evidently, I don't know what the definition of ask is, so I'll inquire of the Lord. Thank you!"

My friend desired to understand. As an educator, she knew there must be more to the definition of asking than she comprehended.

She didn't allow her body of knowledge to override the wisdom offered to her.

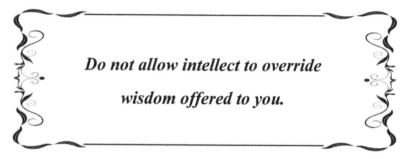

Do not allow intellect to override wisdom offered to you.

I told my friend I would join her and inquire of the Lord as well, and if I heard anything else, I'd let her know. Although I agreed to inquire, I still went about my merry way, thinking I wouldn't hear more about this subject. I believed this was between her and God, He was answering her, and I had been obedient on my end.

As it turned out, it was a three-fold setup. The Lord wanted to answer her.

He wanted to set me up to A.S.K. And you (yes, you) have been set up to receive. Isn't that great news?

This book is intended to bring clarity to the process of asking. While receiving God-given instruction on the process of asking, you'll discover the principles (set things). When you discover these principles, please practice them. Practice will cause the process (movement) of asking to be clear and more direct.

When you ask the biblical way, it will make your soul, which consists of your emotions and intellect, glad. It's almost like updating your emotions, so they won't be caught off guard. Your intellect becomes informed early, so you can do less guessing and avoid unnecessary frustration. No more feelings of false hope leading to disappointments. You'll have the wisdom to receive what you desire because you will have learned to A.S.K.

Let's pray!

God, I have determined in my heart to believe You. I may not understand it all yet, but I do know if I am willing, You will teach me Your ways through Your word. It will cause me to prosper. I believe you, and I give You the freedom to help me in the areas where there is unbelief.

Forgive me for the times I doubted You. I agree with the plan You have for my life. Help me to be closer to You, so I may recognize Your ways and avoid missteps.

I ask that You open up my understanding. I will seek You for information. And I will knock on the areas in my life to which You direct me. Thank You for illuminating Your Word to me. I believe it is done. And when I get the victory, I will give You the glory. In Jesus's name, Amen!

Chapter 1

Asking Amiss

amiss: /əˈmis/ not quite right; inappropriate or out of place.

ONE DAY, THE LORD TOLD ME TO CALL MY SISTER, who lives out of state, and tell her He'd heard her when she asked Him, "God, where are you? Do you hear me asking you about this?" Today, He was answering.

This phone call is your answer. The reason why you have not received an answer yet is you are asking incorrectly. You really have not asked me. You are looking for a new job that will pay well according to your degree so you can make yourself debt-free. Your motive for asking Me for a better job is wrong.

"I know this already," my sister responded, "but I am fed up with this job; with all these degrees, I know I can get a better job than this. I've asked the Lord what He wants me to do and every time I go to look for a job I feel it is not the right thing to do. And I still have outbursts every now and then asking God - am I supposed to be working a job or do you want me to start a business?"

I went on to tell her, "You want to get creditors off your back, and in your mind, the solution is your education, but God wants you to know that He is your Source. He makes you debt-free with or without a job; it is not the job!" A lot of times we forget because of the pressure and the Lord reminds us, *"I am your source."*

James 4:3 says, "Ye ask, and receive not, because ye ask amiss, that ye may consume it upon your lusts." Remember when you ask God for something, you must include Him in the decision-making. Ask God what His desire is. Psalm 37:4-5 says, "Delight thyself also in the Lord: and He shall give thee the desires of thine heart. Commit thy way unto the Lord; trust also in him; and he shall bring it to pass." When you trust God and commit your ways to Him, this is the same as consulting with Him. When you are committed to Him and you trust Him, you will not have an issue with doing it His way, knowing He brings it to pass.

In order to have God's participation, consult Him to avoid moving under your own ingenuity. God wants us to know, "I Am willing to deliver but I will not have other gods before Me (including a job or a degree)."

"Let Me be your Source." "Let Me help you be debt-free but allow Me to do it My way."

Once my sister and I were done conversating. No one was angry or offended because we knew it was God. I couldn't have known what transpired between God and her any other way. I knew her conversation with Him, the questions she asked, and scriptures she used because He was answering.

Let me ask you, reader, a question. The things you're learning or going to school for, do you want to be great at them? Forget great. Are you willing to exercise discipline to master them? That's the real question. Whatever you set out to do, if you practice discipline— something we all have a measure of—you can succeed. But are you willing to practice discipline when it comes to asking God for what you need and desire? There's more to asking than requesting something from someone and waiting to receive it from them. That's not the true definition of ask.

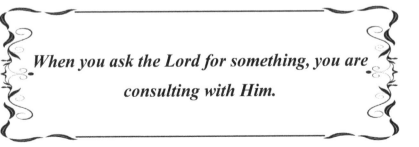

When you ask the Lord for something, you are consulting with Him.

To consult means to seek information or advice from someone with expertise in an area. This means when you make a request, you wait for a response from the expert. God is our expert in all we need and is skilled in getting the information to us. You see, there are times we want the Lord to do things for us, but we have set in our minds how it should be done and what the process should look like. God may have a different view on how He wants to deliver; He looks at the big picture. For example, He wants you to be debt-free so you can assist someone else in becoming debt-free too.

This may require showing others what He did for you so they can believe and experience His love and deliverance too. God may decide to use your job, or He may not. Do not box God in and limit Him to your job or how much knowledge you have. That would really be selling yourself short.

I spoke to my sister several months later, and she told me, since the last time we'd spoken, her husband's job had cut his hours. And although she knew her situation should have gotten worse with that hardship, it was the opposite.

She didn't know how it happened, other than God, but all her bills were being paid, and she was paying off debt faster than she had when they had more money coming in. I told her I knew how. It wasn't a hardship but a Godship.

Stay on His ship. It will always take you in the right direction. Keep following His instructions, and He will get you to the other side, but He wants to do it His way.

We (and that means me too) often map out the conclusion of a situation, and when it doesn't go the way we envision, we give up. We don't ask God for directions. It reminds me of when my husband and I first got married. We would be on our way to a party, and if he couldn't find the location, he'd get frustrated. This was before we had fancy GPS at our fingertips. It was a well-known joke that men typically went in circles for some time before pulling to the side and asking for directions. My husband would drive around for so long and then finally say, "Forget it. I'm going home." I'd reply, "I don't understand. Why can't we pull into a gas station and ask someone?"

We do the same thing with God—speed down the highway with limited directions. We refuse to stop where we are, pull to the side, and ask God for more detailed directions.

We assume our failure means God denied our request. Nope! He had nothing to do with it. We don't think to consult with Him because we think we already know the answers. Anytime we attempt to complete a thing under our own ingenuity, we tend to think we've come to the end of our hope when things don't go as planned. Decide today to accept the Lord's help. Allow Him to deliver you His way.

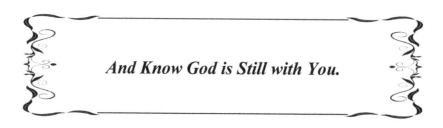

And Know God is Still with You.

Sometimes, we feel like the Lord isn't with us, but even in those times, He is. He's always with you and promised to never leave. However, there are times when He waits for you to decide if you'll follow His instructions or your own.

So how do you change this? Acknowledge Him! "In all thy ways acknowledge him, and he shall direct thy paths" (Proverbs 3:6). This simply means ask Him.

The scripture says to acknowledge Him in all your ways. It doesn't matter how big or small the concern is;

be sure to consult the Lord regardless. This way, you can eliminate some mistakes. Even though your concern may seem easy to address, I guarantee you He has a better way to resolve it and His way comes with peace. And that peace includes time and money, something I know firsthand.

Anyone who knows me knows, when I go shopping, I do not pay full price the majority of the time. When I see something I like, I consult the Lord *first*. If I hear Him say, *Not now*, no matter how bad I want it, I won't buy it. Weeks or months later, remembering my desire, I'll go back to the same store, and lo and behold, the outfit I wanted is now fifty to eighty percent off. No matter how small a decision may be, if you consult Him in all you do, it can save you time and money.

Many times, we don't take things to God in prayer because we think they're not a big deal, but the enemy counts on you to make that decision. Have you ever watched boxing and wondered to yourself, "Why do they keep throwing those small, insignificant punches?" I know I have. But the real question is: are they really insignificant? These small punches are known as jabs, but you may not realize those jabs are wearing on the opponent's body. The enemy uses this same strategy.

He tries to wear you down with the small things so, when he comes in for the kill (or the thing that makes you quit), the size won't matter. Big or small, it could be the last straw for you.

Don't get me wrong. We all make plans in our hearts; however, God directs our actions while moving in those plans (Prov.16:9). Your plan may be to go left, but He may direct you to make a sharp right. You must be willing to trust Him. Keep in mind the plans He has for you are good. "His plan is to prosper you and not to do you harm. His plans are to give you hope and a future." (Jer. 29:11)

Even the boxer with all his skills needs to consult his coach at the end of each round. The coach lets the boxer know if he made any mistakes and how to avoid making them again. In that same setting, he advises him on how to approach the next round. He encourages him and builds up his confidence. We should be asking God, "Did I make any missteps? How should I handle this next round? I know what I can do, God, but is this the best move?"

Lay out your plans before Him, and take His advice. At times, you may have prayed about a thing and still didn't know if you'd heard an answer. Prayer time isn't always a time for asking.

Sometimes, your personal prayer time can be labeled as complaining, venting, whining, or even questioning what He has already said. Please know going to God and asking Him the same thing, over and over, doesn't show you trust Him. You don't need to present your case to Him again. After you ask, follow up with thanksgiving and praise, believing it is already done.

Before taking anything to God in prayer, make sure you first believe. You may wonder how can you do that. Well, I'm glad you asked. When I want to ask God for something, I first find scripture on what I'm believing for and meditate on it. When issues come up that are contrary to what His Word has promised me, I respond to it by saying what His Word has said about it; this agrees with Him. *The model prayer always agrees with God.* And what if I don't believe? If you don't believe the Word of God will assist you with that. Through it, you can educate yourself, on what it means to not accept disbelief and trust God only. You do not have to stress to get there. Let's look at the words believe and agree for a moment.

To believe means to trust, consider, imagine, or think. I find those synonyms interesting because if a man *thinks* on a thing long enough, he's not only capable of believing it but also of becoming it.

Proverbs 23:7 says, "For as he thinketh in his heart, so is he." So if you take what God has said to you and continually think on it, after a while, you will believe it. Consistently meditating on what God says produces the ability to believe and ultimately brings you to a place of trusting what He says. Once this is done, you're ready to go to Him in prayer or agree with Him.

To agree means to approve or say yes. That is so good! It lets you know that to agree with God all you have to do is approve (accept) it and say yes! He won't force His will upon you even when He knows it is best. He has given you free will to choose.

Now you can put your trust (to believe) in the Word of God and your acceptance (to agree) with what God said and act on it. Without strain, you can pray back to Him what you've been meditating on. **Be aware that every new direction in your life will require a new yes from you.** There are some things heaven has been awaiting your permission to move on.

Let me clarify. In the midst of meditating on the Word of God and moving in your plans, still go to Him. Consult Him, daily, on how to meditate and develop your belief.

I know I do. While sharing your plans and desires with God, don't get impatient because impatience can cause you to miss what's for you. God's not waiting for perfection, surety, or a particular timeline; He simply desires you do it His way.

God's way has a method. If you fail to consult Him and you're impatient, if you don't acknowledge Him and you're doubting, you're asking amiss. While asking amiss can mean you missed the mark, it's not cut and dry in every situation. There are times when you can experience a faulty point while on the right road. In other words, you may have missteps while headed in the right direction. Your thought patterns could have caused the misstep. So be clear and know why you are asking.

I pray the Holy Spirit will guide you in every situation as you request His assistance. Amen.

NOTES

Chapter 2

Why Are You Asking?

WHEN I MOVED OUT OF THE HOME WHERE I GREW UP and into my own place, shopping for dinnerware was my jam. If it wasn't in the color or the style, I was looking for, I would have the sales representative search the stockroom, especially if the dinnerware was on sale. Ironically, I never dined from any of it. I had convinced myself I was saving all that dinnerware for the right time. I put the dishes in the cabinet and never pulled them out again. I became a dinnerware collector, purchasing most of it based on other people's opinions of what a nice home should have. I eventually gave most of it away when I realized I didn't really want it. I'd learned to enjoy life in the moment instead.

Remember James 4:3 says, "Ye ask, and receive not, because ye ask amiss, that ye may consume it upon your lusts." In other words, you don't get what you ask for because your motives are self-centered.

Regardless of what your requests entail, ask yourself these four questions:

1.   Why am I requesting this?

2.   What are my motives?

3.   How do I obtain it?

4.   What is the purpose of what I seek to obtain?

Why am I requesting this? Knowing your why allows you to remain sensitive and eliminate asking amiss. When the answer doesn't come right away, don't be tricked into thinking God doesn't hear you, or even worse, He doesn't love you. There's nothing wrong with wanting something. Psalm 23:1-2 says, "The Lord is my shepherd; I shall not want. He maketh me to lie down in green pastures: he leadeth me beside the still waters." This indicates there is nothing wrong with having wants. As your Shepherd, He provides for your wants. "Still waters" indicate His provision comes with peace. No stress, no struggle, no worries, just resting and trusting in Him.

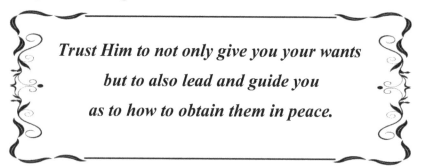

Trust Him to not only give you your wants but to also lead and guide you as to how to obtain them in peace.

What are my motives? Asking amiss means you ask incorrectly but it could also mean you don't have because you ask with the wrong motive. When you know why you're asking and agree to let God provide your wants in peace, you have no anxiety and your motives are made clear. You have a direct aim in mind, and nothing in life is impossible for you to accomplish. You don't plan your life according to how others feel or view you in this space.

Caring about how someone else might view you can cause you to detour from the plans God has for you and miss doors of opportunities. Subconsciously being embarrassed about who you are will not only change your behavior but also your path and even your motives. Ill-driven, your reason for asking becomes all about making you look good instead of focusing on obedience to God. When you focus on pleasing God, your motives remain transparent and cause Him to respond.

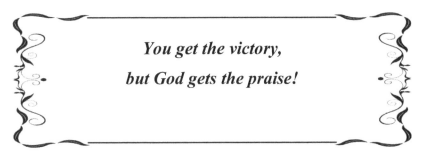

You get the victory,
but God gets the praise!

I heard the Lord say, "Your name is known, but My name is greater." It's not about you. It's about Him in you. This truth is vital because it will give you the strength to remove limitations you may have unconsciously created and limitations people place on you with their opinions. Remember you can do all things through Christ who strengthens you (Phil 4:13). Allow that to be your drive. His strength will get you where you need to go and assist you in accomplishing those impossible things while you give Him glory.

You may be wondering who thinks this way. Many people already understand this and think this way, and they're extraordinarily successful because of it. It's just as easy for you to do, when you implement a change in your heart and mind. Proverbs 23:7 says, "For as he thinketh in his heart, so is he." Keep thinking in this manner until results follow. This isn't the power of positive thinking; this is the power of your belief in God.

How do I obtain what I desire? In order to get answers and favorable responses from the Lord you have to be willing to adjust your mind to His Word. If it's in His Word or you heard Him say it to you, then it's His will.

Don't be the one who only goes to Him for things. Be the one who asks for life-altering changes—a better outlook on life, a new attitude, reconciliation in your family, or peace of mind. Then, find a scripture that supports what you asked for and believe it's for you.

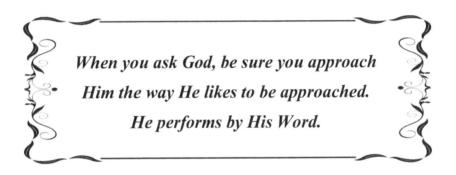

When you ask God, be sure you approach Him the way He likes to be approached. He performs by His Word.

Did you know there's a correct way to approach God? He said to come boldly before the throne of grace, but too often, we stop there. If you continue to read, the latter part of that scripture reads, "that we may obtain mercy and find grace to help in time of need" (Heb. 4:16).

When you seek mercy, you don't come with a sense of arrogance, and you don't come disrespectfully. That's not what boldly means. On the other hand, you don't approach God while you're throwing yourself a sorrowful pity party or feeling worthless.

You obtain His promises by coming with confidence, knowing you will receive forgiveness and power to assist you in your time of need.

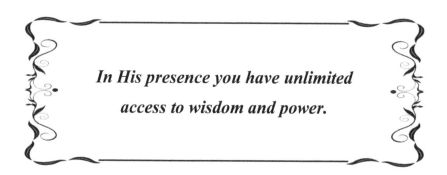

In His presence you have unlimited access to wisdom and power.

What is the purpose of what I seek to obtain? Have you ever wanted something, and once you got it, you realized having it really didn't matter? Have you ever considered the reason why you asked for it in the first place? Know you're important with or without money or things. Things don't determine who you are or your value. We hear this often, but it's important to believe it. Being in His presence helps us renew and adjust our minds in order to receive.

Giving Him the glory encompasses more than glorifying His name so other people come to know who He is. Being blessed and well taken care of yourself also brings glory to your Father, God.

Even getting a new car glorifies Him when God has blessed you with it. Let your Father provide for you, so your blessing can be a witness to others.

Psalm 23 tells you He is your shepherd, and so you don't have to want for anything, but if you read a little further, you see 'He restores my soul: he leadeth me in the paths of righteousness for his name's sake". Sometimes what you experience in life can be traumatic. It could cause your mind to slip, but because He restores your soul (mind, intellect, and emotions), you're covered in His peace. He helps you keep it together. That thing that could have taken your mind, He kept you and helped you to stay in right relationship with Him. It's for the sake of His name, that you and others may know He is good. He is a Father who cares for us and the things that concern us. He wants us to trust Him and come to Him as our Father.

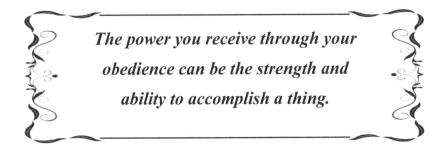

The power you receive through your obedience can be the strength and ability to accomplish a thing.

When you enter His presence and remain, you can get the information you need to reach your desired outcome. When the Lord gives you information coupled with instructions, do not fight His method. If you're seeking mercy, be willing to receive compassion, forgiveness, grace, and power to assist you in your time of need. And you have to do it with boldness (be courageous) to receive all of that from your Father who loves you.

Come on say it with me: I will not cut out the process. I will receive instructions from my Father, and with every victory, I will give Him the glory!

I pray your heart will be changed, and your motives will be right. Amen!

NOTES

Chapter 3

Mix it with Faith

MOST OF US THINK ASKING FOR SOMETHING FROM God shouldn't require a process. No steps involved. And when a process is required, it challenges our faith. Your faith is a vital part of the asking process. Normally, we think, "God gave me a promise, so I'll sit back and wait for Him to bring it to pass, absolutely no movement required." Many of us came up in an era when we were encouraged to "name it and claim it" or "blab it and grab it," but no one told us what we were supposed to grab it with. Are we supposed to do something to take hold of what we want?

It does require movement. Something is supposed to happen in between blabbing and grabbing. Hebrews 4:2 says, "For unto us was the gospel preached, as well as unto them: but the word preached did not profit them, not being mixed with faith in them that heard it." The keyword in this verse, "mixed," indicates you have to act. You can't sit on the Word and expect it to prosper you as it prospers someone else simply because you both heard it,

The scripture says the word preached did not profit them because they didn't mix it with faith. They heard it and took no action on what they heard.

Maybe they didn't know how to use the word preached to get what they needed. And maybe you don't either. But when you consult with the Lord, He will always give you a process to show you how to work with the Word. His process helps you mix your faith with His Word to produce promise.

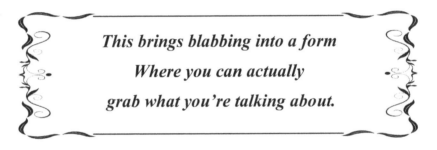

This brings blabbing into a form
Where you can actually
grab what you're talking about.

In chapter one, we defined belief and agreement. Now let's add faith to the mix. The Bible tells us your faith without works is dead (James 2:17). You can believe, but if you don't get up and act on what you believe, you will not obtain your beliefs. You have to do something with what you believe, or it just becomes a strong dream. Your receptiveness to instructions from the Holy Spirit and your obedience after you've made your request known to the Lord are essential to the process if you want results. This is just as we follow daily, real-world processes to obtain predictable outcomes.

One day, I needed to clean my bathtub, and I was dreading it. I didn't feel like prepping my chemicals and smell-goods. I didn't feel like figuring out which musical mood I was in. And most importantly, I didn't feel like scrubbing. Cleaning the tub was an energy exerting task, but it had to be done. Stalling, sitting on the side of the tub, out of curiosity, I turned the can of cleaner around and read the back. At first glance, I read the usual, sprinkle and scrub. But as I continued stalling—I mean reading—I realized, for years, I'd skipped a step, thus making my cleaning process harder than it should have been.

The instructions went something like this. To clean and deodorize: For most problems, sprinkle the bathroom cleaner on a wet surface or sponge, let sit for one minute, rub, and rinse.

Wait a minute. All those years, I was supposed to let the bathroom cleaner sit and then rub, not scrub? Slightly doubting the manufacturer's instructions, I wet the surface and let the cleaner sit for about five minutes. As I rubbed, the dirt effortlessly disappeared.

I was amazed. Going forward, I know the three-step process: sprinkle, set, and rub. Looking at a finished work with redeemed time, I realized I struggled with some things in my life simply because I didn't follow the instructions, including those given to me in His Word.

Why did I doubt the Creator's instructions? There were times I told the Lord, "I hear You, but let's do it this way instead. I'm listening when it comes to this, God, but not when it comes to that." Now I never said those things out loud, but my actions said them. The reality is a process can be a wonderful thing if we embrace the process He gives us for each promise.

This is why Jesus questioned the disciples' faith when He was asleep in the boat during the storm (Matt. 8:26). God expects us to act on what we know. The disciples knew He was a miracle worker. They saw Him turn water to wine (John 2:1-11). They experienced a miracle of abundance when they moved on His word. Their abundance was so great that it overflowed into other people lives. (Luke 5:4-11). And we all experience deliverance time and time again (I Cor. 15:57). The disciples had personal testimonies, as we do, and yet they doubted He would do it again.

They didn't act on what they already knew, the same way we don't always act on what we already know about God.

Changing from doubt to belief is a decision. You have to be willing to say, "God I am going to agree with you that this can be done even if I don't see how I'm going to do it Your way." Then choose a scripture to meditate on and allow faith to come while confessing it. Obey God's voice in order to keep your faith active and alive.

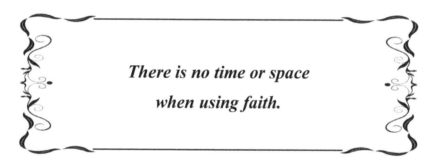

There is no time or space when using faith.

Hebrews 11:1 says, "Now faith is the substance of things hoped for, the evidence of things not seen." Faith is always now. It is not becoming. If there's a struggle, then faith is not yet present.

Faith is the substance (the material in its purest form) of the thing you're hoping for. Although what you're believing for doesn't appear automatically in the natural, as some of us think it should, it does exist, in its purest form, in the spirit.

So how do we obtain it in the natural? I'm glad you asked. When we speak the Word of God on our situation, it creates a frame around what we're believing for and causes faith to come (Hebrews 11:3).

When a housing development is being built, you may not see the homes at first, but you know they're coming because you see the framework. Once the frame is up, then it's time for the material to come. Mixing faith with the Word of God works the same way. The Word of God frames what we are believing for. Once the frame is up, it's time for the material to arrive. Faith comes by hearing and hearing by the Word of God (Romans 10:17). Faith is the material that arrives for what was framed by the Word. Now it's time to start acting on your evidence even though it's not yet seen.

Don't look at this as complicated because you don't yet understand the process of it. It's not complicated. View this development as a means to get it done.

I pray that you take God at His word and recognize faith when it comes. The Lord will guide you as you speak His word and when everything is complete, you'll enjoy the fruit of your labor. Amen!

NOTES

Chapter 4

Don't Cut Out the Process

THERE'S A METHOD TO WHERE YOU'RE TRYING TO GO. In this life, there are steps to everything you do, from obtaining a degree to baking a cake. When you study to obtain a degree, you receive a syllabus at the beginning of each semester, so you know what to expect. You learn how to handle the information and the results your actions yield as they come. Baking a cake requires you to ensure all the ingredients—flour, milk, eggs, baking powder, butter, and sugar—aren't just available but are used. There are requirements to meet, procedures to follow.

When you're looking for a job, first, you fill out an application. If (and I do mean if) your application is accepted, you'll likely be interviewed and tested. If you're hired, you may go through an onboarding orientation. And here is where the expectation increases.

At the orientation, even though you've proven yourself, you need to identify yourself with the required documents, such as a driver's license and social security card. And let us not forget the training. Once this is completed, you're still subject to a ninety-day probation period. These steps are never questioned in the natural; as a matter of fact, you enjoy the hiring process because you're in expectation. So why do you question steps when it comes to spiritual things? You should be enjoying the process, and you should be in expectation.

As children, when we asked permission to go somewhere, we went through some steps. We cleaned our room, dressed appropriately, and had all the pertinent information about the event in hopes we'd be granted a yes from our parents. Oh, but when we made our request known, their process began: a series of the same questions asked in different ways. Back in my day, stories and awkward pauses were designed to check for omissions. Our parents could sense when we were leaving out something. It was all part of the process.

And now I turn the corner. (That's a Canaan Church saying we use when our practical examples are superseded by spiritual principles.) Can you tell me why we think the things of God are any different? It's because we've been tricked into not practicing the process. We think the process delays us in reaching our destination.

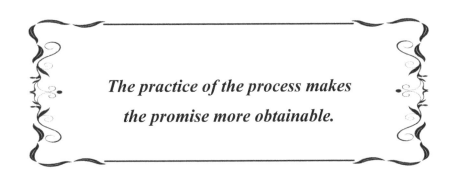

The practice of the process makes
the promise more obtainable.

If you adjust your mind to the practice of the process, nothing will be impossible. Remember even Jesus followed a process and God won't require what is unbearable. He won't exceed your capacity (1 Cor. 10:13). If it appears to be too much to bear, He will take that thing and break it down for you in steps. Do you remember when Jesus fed the five thousand with two fishes and five loaves of bread (Luke 9:13-17)?

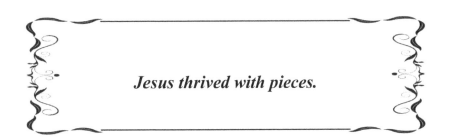

Jesus thrived with pieces.

Luke 9:13-14 says, "But he said unto them, Give ye them to eat. And they said, We have no more but five loaves and two fishes; except we should go and buy meat for all this people. For they were about five thousand men. And he said to his disciples, Make them sit down by fifties in a company."

Notice His first step was to break them into groups of fifty. Have you heard the saying "united we stand, divided we fall"? It wasn't the people Jesus had an issue with but the limited pieces. He was dividing the lack. United, the people stood in lack (hungry at five thousand strong),
but divided into groups of fifty, they were fed and the issue of lack fell. Anything broken into smaller pieces will give your mind a different perspective on how to accomplish it. *I am only trying to feed fifty people at a time.* You can use this process to eliminate lack—but that's another book.

Luke 9:15 goes on to say, "And they did so, and made them all sit down." Why is that so important? Making them sit down is Jesus's second step; He put the issue under His feet. When you magnify God, He gets bigger in your situation and the issue gets smaller.

"Then he took the five loaves and the two fish, and looking up to heaven, he blessed them, and brake, and gave to the disciples to set before the multitude" (Luke 9:16).

Looking to the heavens is acknowledging the Lord and allowing Him to direct your path. You cannot go wrong when you do this, and you are guaranteed it will be more than enough.

Luke 9:17 reads, "And they did eat, and were all filled: and there was taken up of fragments that remained to them twelve baskets." Jesus completed His process to the point of overflow.

Consider this for a moment. There are times we think the Lord hasn't answered yet when, in fact, He has. However, it may have come in a different form than we expected. In the Kingdom of God, it could come in seed form, and what do we know about seeds (Matthew 13)?

Seeds are smaller than the fruit we want and look nothing like what we desire, but they will grow into what we expect them to be. When we make a request unto God, He may hand us a seed, and that seed, at times, is in the form of information. I cannot stress enough that the same way we apply this to our natural lives with no problem is the same way we have to shift our minds and do this with the spiritual part of our lives. Do you think it's a coincidence you're reading about asking or that we examined Jesus walking out a process? These aren't coincidences in your life.

Now is the time to seek the Lord with the information you received. Ask Him why He's showing you this and what you're supposed to do next.

I pray that your asking will cause you to seek, and your seeking will lead you to the place where you need to knock. Amen.

LET'S PAUSE

While reading this book it is okay to pause between pages and learn how to practice thinking God's way. Soak in the scriptures mentioned, over a few days, until you feel in your heart what God is saying about you is true.

This is how you will know this truth is for you:

>He loves you (Psalms 36:7 / John 3:16)

>He cannot lie (Numbers 23:19 / Titus 1:2)

Then ask yourself the following:

1. Do I believe what I just read?
2. Am I willing to ask God about things I don't understand?
3. When I get an answer, am I willing to follow His advice?

There will absolutely be times where a small adjustment is needed. So, what! Thank God there is still time.

I pray that you will recognize when an adjustment needs to be made and pride will not stop you from repenting and experiencing all the things God has for you. Amen.

NOTES

Chapter 5

ASK

ask: /ask/ request or seek (someone) to do or give something (like an answer or some information); the biblical, three-step process—ask, seek, knock—to obtain within the Kingdom of God.

And this is the confidence that we have in him, that, if we ask any thing according to his will, he heareth us. 1 John 5:14

ASKING GOES BEYOND REQUESTING PERMISSION TO receive something you desire or need from God. To ask biblically is a three-step-process. This process isn't designed to make things complicated in your life but to cause things to be completed. Let's take a closer look at this process; for the sake of clarity, I'll use the word *request* in the place of ask. When we make a request to the Lord, we've begun the asking process, but we have more to do.

Many of us have been satisfied with "I asked the Lord and now I wait," hoping He hands us what we want. That isn't the correct definition of asking.

The Lord has an attitude of "ask me, and see won't I do it", but if you are anything like me, you might think, "I have already prayed about this, why haven't I heard from the Lord yet? We talked about this already!" Technically, you have not. Imagine God hearing you make a request and watching you sit back to wait on Him.

God: What did they say?

Angels: We're not sure. They walked by mumbling something!

> ***Asking is a three-step process.***
> ***It does not start and end with your request.***
> ***There are further steps to complete.***

You may feel you've spent time asking, but the Word says you have not because you ask not (James 4:2). It goes on to talk about how most of us try to make it happen on our own. Therefore, a lot of arguments happen between us. We, as people, want things, and we fight to get them and still do not have them.

There's no doubt the Lord has something better; all you have to do is ask. Why not ask Him for what He wants you to have and seek further instructions on how to obtain it? I'm sure it's bigger and better than what you could ever plan for your situation or your life.

In the introduction, I shared how my discovery of the A.S.K. process came about. I was inquiring of the Lord for my friend in addition to the instructions I had already followed to give her a message from Him. Well, He gave me more. I was reading Matthew 7:7, and something within the text stood out to me. I had never seen it before. Instead of reading across, my eyes were automatically reading *diagonally*. I knew the Spirit of God was revealing something in His Word to me. I had read this passage before, but I had never seen what I'm about to share with you, nor had I heard it before.

Matthew 7:7 reads, "**Ask,** and it shall be given you; **seek**, and ye shall find; **knock,** and it shall be opened unto you." But I was seeing it like this:

Ask, and it shall be given.

Seek, and ye shall find.

Knock, and the door shall be opened.

As I read further, I noticed each sentence started with one of the letters in the word *ask* and they were in order: A.S.K. It was an abbreviation made up of the first letter of three words to form one word. And here was the proof in plain sight. Then I heard God. *It's not a coincidence ask is spelled this way. It's not just a word. It's an acronym.*

I was stunned. I had to stop what I was doing and look up the word *acronym* even though I knew the meaning. I couldn't find the definition fast enough. As I searched, I thought, "If I'm hearing correctly, God, you are revealing a mystery to me. And I'm grateful. The first step is to ask, the second step is to seek, and the third step is to knock. They all require action. The action that can clear up any missteps and change the way we communicate with You."

What you don't know, you just don't know. This is why it's so important to lay your plans out and consult Him on everything you do. When you consult Him, He reveals things to you.

An acronym is an abbreviation formed from the initial letters of other words and pronounced as a word (NASA is an example). I wondered why I hadn't seen A.S.K. in the Scripture after all this time.

I allowed it to be hidden in plain sight, I heard the Lord say. *It is the Spirit of Truth revealing more truth to you. I am introducing a kingdom principle to you* (John 16:12-13).

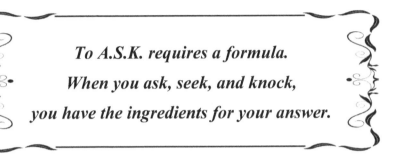

To A.S.K. requires a formula.
When you ask, seek, and knock,
you have the ingredients for your answer.

Do you remember in school when your math formulas used symbols, like an equal sign with two or more variables representing values? In this case, we have three variables and our variables are the letters a, s, and k. Each variable stands for a value of great importance, but most often, we only use one.

When Holy Spirit revealed the truth of A.S.K, I was honored to know He was ready to lead me into more and more that would include all the variables. The Spirit of the Lord wants to answer all our inquiries and show us more truth.

I heard the Lord say to me one day, *"No more type and shadow." "This is the time of manifestation."* In the Old Testament we have types and shadows. Types are an example, or a pattern, modeling something of the future. Shadows showed us truth coming, which was Jesus Christ. Both are spiritual realities fulfilled through His life in the New Testament. God doesn't want us to continue to read about examples and things to come, but like Christ, He wants us to be living examples, of Him and His goodness!

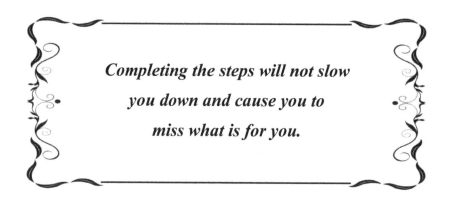

Completing the steps will not slow you down and cause you to miss what is for you.

But I'm telling you: you must be willing to request in the biblical sense. You may not realize it, but you follow a process in almost everything you do in life, and eventually the process becomes second nature to you. Driving is a process. Brushing your teeth involves several steps, but you don't give up on it for obvious reasons.

Be sure to practice these steps until they become second nature and you're able to A.S.K. without thinking about it.

Remember how Jesus fed the five thousand. He **asked** (requested) of the Lord: How would you have me to feed your people? He **sought** instructions on what He was already believing for. Jesus **knocked** and accessed the authority given to Him. What He did looks like this for you. You make a request (**ask**), you seek information on how to complete it (**seek**), and you move on it with full force and no hesitation (**knock**).

The Lord's Prayer demonstrates a pattern too. He said when you pray, do it in this manner. There's a method to everything we do, so let us not be tricked into getting off the roads that would take us to our destinies. These methods will keep us in the place of receiving. Some things (ideas, concepts, and inventions) have your name on them *just* because you requested them. These come from within you.

Let me give you an example. Let's say you request to be debt-free, and when the Lord responds to your request, He responds with an idea. For some time, you stand still in the middle of life, thinking God hasn't answered, when in fact, He has. You finished step one, request. You stopped before step two, seek information regarding the idea He gave you.

And you never acted on step three, knock to gain access to freedom from debt through the idea He gave you. The idea came from within you because it had your name on it.

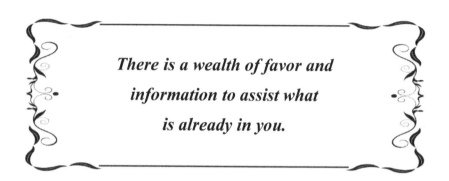

There is a wealth of favor and information to assist what is already in you.

And then there are some things stored up for you. 1 Corinthians 2:9 affirms, "But as it is written, Eye hath not seen, nor ear heard, neither have entered into the heart of man, the things which God hath prepared for them that love him." God has prepared some things for you because you love Him. That is so good! Rest in knowing some things have been made ready in advance for a purpose, and that purpose is you.

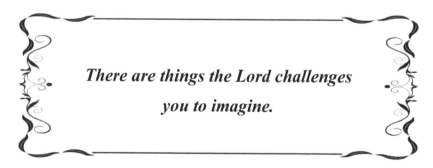

There are things the Lord challenges you to imagine.

You're capable of accomplishing more than you think. Let that sink in. Why? Because Christ can do exceedingly (an unusual degree) abundantly (large quantities) above (surpassing) all you can ask or think, according to the power that works in you (Ephesians 3:20). So be bold enough to ask.

Close your eyes and imagine something you've had on your heart for some time now but haven't requested in this manner yet.

Imagine yourself in what He said to you for one minute. Is it peace in your family? Is it transportation? What does it look like? What kind of car, the color, 2 doors or 4? See yourself in it. Touch the wheel and enjoy the leather seats. If you can see yourself in it, then you can be it. You have unused creativity. It's past time for you to start dreaming again. And understand that whatever you can imagine yourself in, God can do even better. So, Go bigger!

Imagine yourself in what He said to you for three minutes and go bigger (it's the same as having a vision board but instead of looking at the picture you use your imagination and put yourself in it. This time stretch yourself. Go beyond what you consider normal. Imagine yourself in the car, in the house.

Don't just imagine the car, give yourself an upgrade. Sit in it, look at the details. What's the color of the seats? And the stitching? You can even do this to become a better person. Change your attitude and behaviors. What do I want my change to look like?

Pretty amazing, right? Don't forget to write down what you saw (Habakkuk 2:2). And don't ever think anything is too big or too much for you to accomplish. With the help of God, you will accomplish it to an unusual degree, in a larger quantity, surpassing what you can ever request or think. You just have to be willing to include Him in your three-step process.

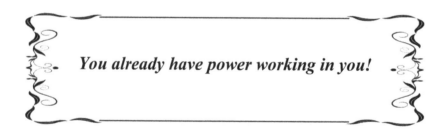

You already have power working in you!

The power working in you is what generated the idea after you asked to be debt-free. God said, *Is that all? I can do bigger and better than that! Let's make you and your entire family debt-free and put you in a place where you can help someone else in need.*

Everyone in their lifetime will have a minimum of one or two million-dollar ideas that could make them rich. I believe that but it's up to you to ask God for the how. Have you ever had an idea for something you've never seen before come to mind. I'm sure you have. (Psst! If you still haven't seen it, that would be your cue to start moving on it before someone else hears the Lord say it and obeys more quickly.) The Lord possesses unlimited riches, and He gives to you out of them.

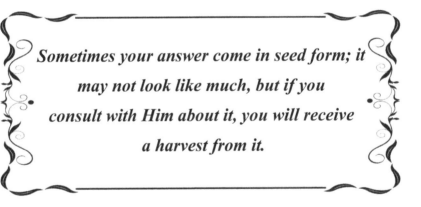

Sometimes your answer come in seed form; it may not look like much, but if you consult with Him about it, you will receive a harvest from it.

God doesn't look at the size of your request. Matthew 21:22 tells us, "And all things, whatsoever ye shall ask in prayer, believing, ye shall receive." Your request can be great or small. The key is to believe *before* you receive your request. Believe in Him, not for the thing. My goodness, that is good!

You should make that one of your daily confessions, as I have. "It's not the things I'm believing for, but it's You, God, I believe in."

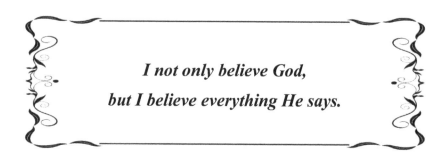

I not only believe God,
but I believe everything He says.

John 16:23-24 states, "And in that day ye shall ask me nothing. Verily, verily, I say unto you, Whatsoever ye shall ask the Father in my name, he will give it you. Hitherto have ye asked nothing in my name: ask, and ye shall receive, that your joy may be full." The scripture did not say you never asked. It says you have asked nothing in His name, which would be the correct way to ask. I figure if we can ask in His name, it must be possible to also ask outside of His name, which would be incorrect and cause us to ask amiss. And asking in His name does not just mean ending your prayer with "in Jesus's name, Amen."

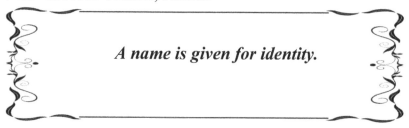

A name is given for identity.

Identity is who you are, what you think about yourself, and the image you project to the world. When you request in His name, it's in His character, image, likeness, authority, and dominion to respond and respond in a big way. Do you remember those WWJD (What would Jesus do?) bracelets?

In every request you submit to God, consider what He would do next:

- What would be His thoughts on the matter?
- How would He respond?
- Do you trust Him enough to know His plans for you are only good?

You cannot go wrong when you believe and accept what He has for you.

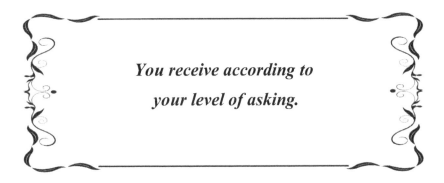

You receive according to your level of asking.

For a proven plan, ensure your request allows His will to be done on earth as it is in heaven (Matthew 6:10). Notice it says it is already done in heaven. When you pray, you're agreeing with what God has already determined to do for you anyway. You cannot go wrong when you agree with what He said and how He wants to do it. He wants you to have what you're requesting as much as you do. You're always good enough and worth it. Starting now, practice requesting of God in prayer, and don't be afraid. Do not be afraid to invite Him into your home, into your petitions, and into your solutions.

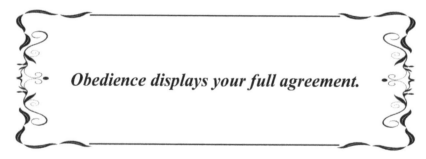

Obedience displays your full agreement.

His invitation can come in different forms, such as the written word (in the form of the Bible), the Word you hear in your ear (as he whispers to you), or even a billboard that sticks with you. Be present to receive your request. And believe you will receive it. After all, He said A.S.K. So ask!

Now, it's time to expect Him, look for Him, and seek Him. Make your requests of the Lord like this: *Please give me your thoughts on this. Help me to know and understand Your ways through Your words, so I can succeed in this area.* Amen.

NOTES

Chapter 6

SEEK

seek: /sēk/ attempt to find something or ask for something from someone; to search or go on a quest for something.

And ye shall seek me, and find me, when ye shall search for me with all your heart. Jeremiah 29:13

SEEK MEANS TO CONSULT, BUT IT ALSO MEANS TO chase down. There comes a time in your life when consulting God turns into desperately seeking after Him with your whole heart. You don't care who sees you or what they think. In this place, you realize consulting Him is the most important thing in your life. You're not only willing to consult with Him, but you're also willing to chase Him down because all your answers lie with Him. Seeking is what happens in between asking and knocking.

Then you're invested in what you believe in. You no longer go by what you see, but you go by what you learn from spending time with Him.

When you truly seek God and His advice, you will make Him a priority, and you won't stop chasing after Him even when you feel fulfilled. Psalm 27:4 reads, "One thing have I desired of the Lord, that will I seek after; that I may dwell in the house of the Lord all the days of my life, to behold the beauty of the Lord, and to enquire in his temple." Do you see that word *enquire*? It means to ask or to find out information from someone. You are supposed to go to Him for information. In Him, you will find every answer you seek.

When I focus on the definition of seeking, it gives me a vision of someone searching for a thing they desperately need or desire. Imagine a person turning over tables and couches to reunite with something or someone he or she has lost. It reminds me of my coworker's search. One day, he came to work saying he'd lost his wedding ring and had no idea where it could be.

"Where did you look?" I asked him. "Did you look in your car or check your pockets?"

"I've looked everywhere, the couch cushions, under it! It's nowhere in the house. My wife is going to kill me. Please tell your husband, Owen, to pray for me."

I told my husband, who said, "Did He ask God? Tell him God will help him find his ring."

I repeated to him what my husband advised, and the next day my coworker came to work smiling because he had found the ring. While it may seem like just a ring to you, it was of high importance to him (and the situation could have ended very differently).

I also had my own experience with searching. One day, while volunteering at a church, I had to run to my car. When I looked outside, it was raining. I needed my coat with a hood on it, but it had been missing for over a year. I was so upset with myself because it was a stylish leather coat with the best lining, which kept me nice and warm. It had a detachable hood, and I had received it as a birthday gift from my husband, who drove five hours on his motorcycle to get it. And then it hit me. Not only did I not take good care of the coat, but I didn't appreciate the sacrifice my husband made when he purchased it for me.

I stopped where I was and asked the Lord to forgive me for not being a good steward of my blessing. Then I asked Him to please return my coat. I said, "God if you return my coat, I promise I will take better care of it" (1 Tim. 6:20). It was time for me to get my act together!

The Lord had me apologize to my husband for not being appreciative, and I did so immediately.

I had no clue where to look for my coat, so I sought God and asked Him what to do next. He instructed me to praise Him. I knew what that meant. I thanked Him for returning my coat before it was returned.

A few weeks later, I was invited to a Grammy party when two of my friends, in a gospel duet, won an award. I really didn't want to go out in the cold, but I didn't want to miss the celebration of this big accomplishment in their lives either. So of course, I went. As the evening progressed, and we mingled and talked to other guests, for some strange reason, we started talking about coats. It was winter, and leather coats were extremely popular, so several people were sporting them.

We discussed what we liked about different styles of leather jackets, and a young lady asked me a question about the leather coat I was wearing. I answered her question and said, "But I used to have a really nice leather coat my husband bought me for my birthday. As a matter of fact, it looked a lot like yours, but I lost it." I went on to identify the intricate lining that made it mine and how I loved some special things about the coat.

"Oh my God!" she said.

"What's wrong" I asked.

"This is your coat!"

At this point, I was a little confused because, even though I knew her husband, I didn't know her well. She said, "Do you remember visiting a church and leaving your coat there? We put it in the bulletin and announced it for months, but no one claimed it. Here, this is your coat!"

I was stunned. I'd grown up in that church, and I visited from time to time, but I hadn't been there in over a year. It hadn't dawned on me to check there. Then, I remembered I must have left it on the back bench when I attended a prayer meeting.

Imagine if I hadn't gone to that party. Do you see how God blessed me and returned to me what was mine after I repented? Wow! I'm still amazed by that moment. My new attitude prevented me from asking amiss. Instead, I made my request, sought Him, and did what I heard in my ear. It was all in God's plan for me to be there and have that conversation with her, and I had focused on Him, not so much the coat.

I heard the Lord say, *Don't ever be afraid to ask. Nothing is ever lost in me* (Psalm 145:18-20).

When you get to the second step, and it's time to seek, you don't have to know how to go about searching for what you've requested. It's also okay if you haven't heard Him give you specific instructions on how to seek. During these times, stay close to Him by consulting Him in everything, and be sure to thank Him before it comes to pass. Present your request to God with thanksgiving (Phil. 4:6). You can thank God for something you're asking Him for because you believe, when you ask, it is already done.

Remember seek not only means to look for something, but it also means to ask for something from someone, as I sought the Lord's help by asking for assistance. Everything you will ever need is in Him. You shouldn't always be focused on your request; if it comes to your mind, tell Him, "thank you," as though it's already done.

When I told the story about my coat, someone asked me, "You took your coat back after she had it in her possession for over a year?" I sure did. The coat never belonged to her. If I hadn't taken back what belonged to me, I wouldn't have completed the covenant I made with God on that rainy day. While I got my act together, the Lord used the young lady to demonstrate good stewardship to me. Why would I refuse to accept what I asked Him to give back?

If your request has been a long time coming, someone else could be looking after it until you get your act together.

If so, don't allow what's yours to become theirs permanently. Don't you dare feel bad when the Lord blesses you and it appears to be taking from someone else.

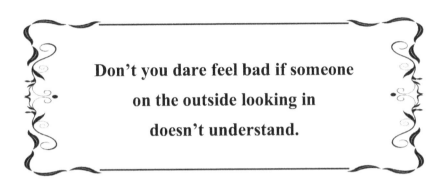

Don't you dare feel bad if someone on the outside looking in doesn't understand.

After all, the Lord is capable of blessing the other person for being a good steward all by Himself. I pray that you will not allow what others think detour you from the will of God. You will acknowledge Him on everything you do, even when you don't understand, and allow Him to direct you. Amen.

NOTES

Chapter 7

KNOCK

knock: /näk/ to strike a sounding blow with the fist, knuckles, or anything hard, especially on a door or window, as when seeking admittance.

For every one that asketh receiveth; and he that seeketh findeth; and to him that knocketh it shall be opened. Matthew 7:8

KNOCKING IS THE THIRD STEP IN THE PROCESS OF ASK and it is all about action. Once you get to this point, you're sure about what you heard from God. Don't apologize for who you are, and don't minimize yourself to make others feel comfortable. You cannot fear failure, nor can you afford to be discouraged at this point. Determine to be unbothered when you look foolish to others. We look foolish in other things, and for some reason, we're okay with that, but when it comes to the things of God, we want to be shy. But no more!

The key to A.S.K.ing is to exercise it, as you would with any other method and don't get mad at God if you haven't been practicing. That's like a doctor getting mad at the hospital because he doesn't know what to prescribe to a patient. It's his responsibility to study and finish his residency. It is the lawyer's responsibility to stay abreast of new laws. She can't get mad at the court because she doesn't know where to begin in her defense. And just like those two professionals have a responsibility, it's your responsibility to study and know the Word in order to A.S.K. properly.

Yes, you're going to make mistakes, but just like lawyers practice law and doctors practice medicine, you have to practice the Word until you get good at it. 2 Timothy 2:15 says, "Study to shew thyself approved unto God, a workman that needeth not to be ashamed, rightly dividing the word of truth." As you do this, when you knock, doors will open for you.

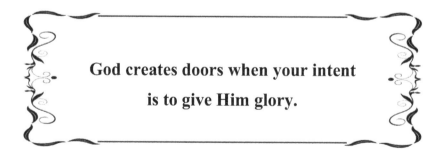

God creates doors when your intent is to give Him glory.

Remember the deal? In your knocking, you get the win and God gets the glory! You get the victory, but the praise and the honor belong to Him. Knocking isn't just about the action itself. It's also about the sound you make when you knock. Is your sound or what you say glorifying Him?

When it's time to knock, follow His instructions to the fullest. Be sensitive to the Spirit of God, and be willing to go all the way. In II Kings 13:19, the king of Israel went to see the prophet, Elisha (who is the voice of God). Elisha instructions to the king was to strike the ground to represent His future victories. The king struck the ground three times and stopped. The prophet got upset at the king and told him you should've knocked more. You can't stop short, thinking there's no more when, in actuality, the victory has just begun. Keep moving in what God has said to you.

One day, my husband said the Lord was going to give him a brand-new Ford Expedition. This model had just come out. The vehicle was popular and expensive, and our money and credit were not in our favor. Good people sometimes come upon bad times. And it was one of those times for us.

Long story short: he went to the dealership to purchase the car, but because of our circumstances, they didn't sell it to him.

They told him, "Mr. Black, we can't help you. Come back when something has changed." The following week, he went back and saw the same salesmen and had the same conversation. "Look, Mr. Black," the salesman told him, "if your credit hasn't changed, and you have no down payment, there's really nothing I can do at this time. Please come back when things have changed."

My husband returned to the dealership every week in this manner until, one day, something changed. This time, the salesman saw him coming and met him at the door. "Hello, Mr. Black. Has anything changed with your credit or your down payment? No? Then there's nothing I can do for you!"

My husband responded, "Okay, see you next week."

The salesman said, "Just one moment. I'll be right back."

Are you taking note of the determination my husband had and his lack of embarrassment? You would think he didn't care about how he looked or what people thought about him—and he didn't.

Do you know why? Because when you know what you heard God say to you, this is what knocking looks like. When you obey God's Word, it causes others to obey God concerning you.

So the salesman came back and said the owner wanted to see my husband. The owner made a phone call to the corporate office. "Listen, I need you to give Mr. Black a loan based on my word," he said. "Use my name for his credit." Then he told my husband, "Mr. Black, go home and wait for us to mail you a check. Bring that check in, and that will be your down payment." A few weeks later we went and picked up our brand-new car. My husband's knocking was his obedience to what he had heard.

Now, even though there are three steps—ask, seek, knock—there will be times when all three steps aren't required. As I studied ask-related scriptures, I noticed semicolons. Going back to my school days, in English class we learned semicolons connect sentences. They link two independent clauses closely related in thought. The semicolon ensures you don't conclude one sentence without including the other. It's there so you will know to pause, but by no means is the action yet completed. The act is not complete until you include them both.

It's the same with Matthew 7:7. Ask, and what shall be given? The manifestation? No, you'll be given the information. You're to take that information and complete the action after the semicolon. Seek; go on a quest. Seek the place where you should be in order to knock and gain access to what you have been believing for.

Matthew 7:7 says, "Ask, and it shall be given you; seek, and ye shall find; knock, and it shall be opened unto you." After realizing the semicolon indicated all three statements work as one, I still asked Holy Spirit about the semicolons.

As I searched for more information under His direction, I looked at the purpose of a semicolon again. When a semicolon is used to join two or more ideas in a sentence, those ideas are then given equal position or rank. Wait a minute.

This means you don't always have to start at step one. There is no "and" after the word *seek* or before the word *knock*. It's not a suggested order. These steps are independent, and any one of the three can start the process. God may tell you to do step three and then step one. Follow His lead. He will not guide you wrong. The definition of a semicolon says these steps have equal rank.

Don't get stressed out trying to remember how to do the steps and in what order. Your steps are ordered by the Lord, and He will instruct you on which step to take first. (Psalms 37:23) My husband's new truck was an example of starting at step one and hopping over to step three without completing step two.

If you're unfamiliar with God's voice, then you should start with step one and ask Him. Be okay with asking God what step to start with. He will either say, "You're in the right place," or, "Move on to step two, and seek me," or "Begin step three, and knock."

God is just good like that! There are times when the Lord tells me to go and knock, and I think "Excuse me? You want me to just go claim what is mine?" But I still obey. Sometimes, you complete steps without even knowing you're doing so when you couple your willingness to obey with fasting and praying.

Notice each action in Matthew 7:8 ends with –eth, I have heard some debate it is not continuously and others interpret this to mean you should keep asking, over and over, and it will eventually be given to you, but that's not necessarily correct either.

You don't have to keep asking God for the same thing. He's not forgetful. Nor do you have to beg Him or hope He'll have pity on you and answer. While the passage says to continue to ask, it's not literal. It refers to repeating a method; if you continue to practice this method, you'll keep getting this result. This isn't meant in the sense of nagging God until you get what you want, like some spoiled kid. It means this is a principle that needs no monitoring. Principles are automatic.

Just like water is always wet and gravity will bring you down, asking will cause you to receive. When you continue to ask, you will continue to receive. Continue to seek, and you will continually get revelation. Continue to knock, and you will continue to get access to the revelation you asked for.

In Matthew 7:9-11, the author no longer mentions seeking and knocking. He simply says ask. Do you know why? There's no need to break it down and explain it again. It was explained in verses 7 and 8 that the word *ask* included all three steps. Therefore, he simply says, "Or what man is there among you who, if his son asks for bread, will give him a stone?

Or if he asks for a fish, will give him a serpent? If you then being evil, know how to give good gifts to your children, how much more will your Father who is in heaven give good things to those who ask Him!"

Just because you feel you know the Word or you heard information from the Lord doesn't mean you know how to act on it yet. Be ready to listen prior to knocking. Hebrews 5 talks about being unskilled in the Word of righteousness. Don't say Amen too quickly. These days, it seems everyone knows the Word or has at least heard it, but everyone doesn't practice it. Then, you have some who practice the Word, but don't know how to use it from a place of righteousness. The Word is letting us know to stay in good relationship with God, so we can use the Word properly.

If you don't know how to use the Word to stay righteous (in right standing with God), we are just as babes even with our, Greek-reading, self-taught, theological selves. And I say self-taught because, often, we won't allow the Spirit of God to teach and lead us because we think we already know. What good is knowing the Word if you're not skilled? I don't mean skilled in teaching and preaching. I mean skilled in bringing it to pass while staying close to Him, the Lord our Righteousness. (Psalms 119:9)

Without a demonstration, you're just talking. You have to know how to use the Word. It's a weapon. You have to know how much to use for your situation, and you must be precise. It is the sword of the spirit, double-edged, which means it cuts coming and going. You can't just go in telling the truth any way because it's true. You can't slam it on the table like dominoes. It's sharp! It's quick! And it's alive! When it pierces, it divides the soul from the spirit so the real you can stand up and declare the truth without hesitation or confusion, but with wisdom. (Hebrews 4:12)

God said it is with love and kindness that He draws us, and He expects us to do the same with our brothers and sisters. When it's time to knock, you will know you have the right to gain access and expect the door to open.

I pray that you will obey God's voice, and have miraculous victories allowing others to witness the power of His love for you and them. Amen.

NOTES

Chapter 8

Change the Way You Think

Think: /THINGk/ to have a particular opinion, belief, or idea about someone or something; to take into consideration; to concentrate; to expect.

THERE IS A MENTAL ATTITUDE OR APPROACH WE should have when making a request of the Lord. In order to move towards success, it's not okay to settle for the norm. We have to know God wants His best for us and be willing to take a different approach. We achieve this by changing the way we think.

Keep in mind, your last thought doesn't have to be your final destination. Earlier, we learned however a man or women continues to think in his or her heart, so they will become. However, everything in your life won't change from a single thought. You must practice this way of thinking.

This doesn't mean you allow anything and everything to run across your mind. When you take time to meditate or think, it has to be on something that brings life. The Word of God is that life, and it aims your thinking at a purpose.

As you begin to follow the 3 step process of A.S.K the Lord will direct you in His word to assist you in making the change.

Let us stop here and practice. Decide on your subject, it could be your desire to change your attitude, the way you view yourself or maybe a career. Think about the details of it. In other words, you want to be in it. Think yourself into what it's supposed to look like with you in it. Maybe you are one who is known for being emotional, which causes you to misunderstand and act too soon. If you want to be the type of person who remains calm, so it will be easier to think of a solution, practice that. See yourself remaining calm, talk to yourself, and answer if needed.

Use the Word of God for your support. Take verses and make confessions out of them. For example, wrath does not produce the righteousness that is from God, and I thank God that I am quick to listen, slow to speak, and slow to wrath. My words are full of grace, seasoned with salt, and I know how to answer every man. (James 1:19-20 and Colossians 4:6) Breathe and respond reasonably.

If it's a career you desire, do your research on it, and begin calling yourself a manager, an author, or a lawyer. See yourself at the desk. Get yourself a filing cabinet and a briefcase, and start moving towards that. I put this in practice when I was not feeling good about who I was or how I looked. Every morning, I would look at myself in the mirror and tell myself how beautiful I was. I became so confident that I began to tell my husband, "Hey, Owen, you know what? Your wife is pretty." "I know," he would respond.

Soon, I didn't have to announce it anymore. I would look up and he would be staring, so I would ask him, "What?" And he would say, "Nothing, you are really pretty. Can I just look at my wife?"

Now here is where it gets really good. We would go out of town to another state or to a local store around the corner, and others would stop me and say, "Excuse me, I just wanted to say you are really pretty." I would kindly thank them, look at my husband in silence, and proceed to walk down the aisle. Ladies and gentlemen, the Lord was giving me confirmation.

The Lord was letting me know your words have power and you can think or speak yourself into what is already for you. I was running into my own confession, and now my thoughts and powerful speaking had become a reality.

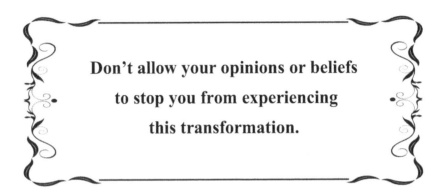

Don't allow your opinions or beliefs to stop you from experiencing this transformation.

Your opinions can be wrong regardless of how long they've been a part of you. Joshua 1:8 says, meditate or think on the Word of God day and night and observe it on purpose. Then, when a concern arises, you will remember the Word of God and make your decision based on it. This will cause you to prosper and make your way successful.

Take into consideration when a process presents itself, it does not have to be a challenge. The A.S.K. process is not a hard thing. This is going to enable you to take it one step at a time, but be careful not to whine and complain. The Holy Spirit is there to guide you every step of the way and instruct you on where to knock.

So, let's walk through every door and get to the other side.

When you're believing God for a job request, concentrate on the position or the role by imagining yourself in the place you're believing for. I am a witness that this works. I started working at a financial institution as a teller and would imagine myself in a supervisor's position. Whenever my coworkers asked for an approval, I initialed their deposits. I was so convinced about what I was believing for, whenever my manager was unavailable, she told the other employees, "Go to Audrey, and have her approve it for you." Although we all laughed, I initialed their work, and they completed the transactions.

One day, I was called into a meeting with the president of the bank. She said, "I'm not sure what kind of God you serve, but all of the district is talking about you. They want to know if you're interested in this new program to train you and prepare you for your own branch."

Not only would I get that supervisor position I desired, but the company was offering me the title and position of president as well. How amazing is God? I went from branch to branch, filling in for branch presidents on leave, evaluating the sales of the branches, and introducing ways to improve customer service and productivity.

I don't know why the president made a statement about the God I served. I hadn't had any conversations with her in regard to my faith. I hadn't told her I was a believer. However, let's be clear. I serve, the one and only, true and living God, and I promised Him I'd always give Him the glory. My life witnessed for Him, and I hadn't even opened my mouth yet.

Before I left the banking industry, my picture was displayed, along with a few others, on a poster in every branch in the Southern California regional area when the bank recognized me among those who exhibited excellent customer service. I walked into a branch and the manger recognize me from the poster. She said, "Do you mind autographing our poster before you leave?" Do you see how God went beyond what I could ask or think? He was making my name great. He gave me the victory, and I gave Him the praise.

If you want more, you have to expect more. Ephesians 3:20 says thinking or meditating on His Word for you is as powerful as asking. Here is some truth. Allow your heart to continue to think on it long enough, and eventually, you will be bold enough to ask and expect results. This is what God wants. It's important you see both your requests and your thoughts bring about results. God wants to do abundantly above for you, but you have to be willing to allow it to exist in your thinking. If you let it exist at least in your imagination, He can come in and make it more than you could ever imagine, but you have to give God something to work with.

God is willing to do more, as illustrated in Isaiah 55, so ask Him, "What else should I be praying. for? I don't want to cut myself short. I know my mind is limited and my thoughts aren't the same as yours, but God, You said, the way rain comes down and waters the Earth is the same way You will supply me with Your Word, so I can increase and grow."

Ask God to give you information about what to pray and what to say. The Lord doesn't want you to worry. He wants you to know that, as a Father, He not only loves and cares for you but wants you to trust Him for your provision. He understands your needs and your wants.

Philippians 4:6-7, says, "Be careful for nothing; but in everything by prayer and supplication with thanksgiving let your request be made known unto God. And the Peace of God, which passeth all understanding, shall keep your hearts and minds through Christ Jesus."

When I read the Word, I love to pose questions to get a better understanding of the text. Remember the Holy Spirit is present to teach you, so ask away. In this case, I wanted to know what I should guard my heart from?

The answer is to guard it from worry. This passage says not to be full of care regarding anything. Don't be in a state of mind in which you are troubled.

The scripture doesn't say not be responsible. It says not to be full of worry or anxiety, and it tells you how to cancel out that state of mind. In everything, when you are requesting from God, be sincere in your communication with Him. Ask for what you want, and include some thanksgiving. When you thank God for what you're asking before you see it, not in fear or worry but with sincere praise, this shows God you trust Him. And it will cause His peace to cover your heart and cover your mind from worry and anxiety. This is a position of expectation.

Communicate with God in everything. Nothing is too big or too small, too horrible or shameful. When He answers, it may be with a principle. When He gives you a principle to work, don't try to manually manifest the promise. The result of a principle is automatic, and He watches over His own word to perform it.

However, He wants you to agree to allow miracles to break out in your life. Stay in agreement with God. Know that what you're asking Him will take place. Remember He loves you and He will not lie.

I pray that your way of thinking will be changed, and it will not keep you from experiencing miracles. You are in expectation and will allow God to show you more. Amen.

NOTES

Chapter 9

Understand His Ways

UNDERSTANDING THE WAYS OF GOD MAKES ALL THE difference in the three-step A.S.K. process. When we misinterpret what's taking place, misunderstandings arise and try to keep us from going to God, our loving Father. Have you ever experienced a misunderstanding due to differences in upbringings, cultural differences, or a simple gesture? I have. What meant one thing to me meant something different to someone else. God is the same way. His understanding is different from ours. His perspective on things will always be broader with a known end in mind. The Bible gives us a picture of how different our ways are from God's; as high as the heavens are from the earth, that is how high His thoughts and ways are from ours (Isaiah 55:9).

I was talking to my godson one day, and he said, "People say God works in mysterious ways, but that's not true. The mysterious part comes in because they don't understand His ways."

That is so true, but it doesn't have to be that way. We have access to God's thoughts through His Word.

Because He loves us, He's willing to let us know how He thinks and works. He only asks us to come into agreement with what He's saying and doing, and we will see those things come to pass. In the same way the rain and snow water the earth and cause it to grow (Isaiah 55:10), His Word will have an effect on us and cause us to grow. His Word will not come back to Him void, but it will accomplish what He has sent it to do. God says it *will*, not it might.

God's way is patient, as we see in the story of Moses and the children of Israel. If you know this story, you know God delivered them from generations of captivity. Pharaoh released them, but then he changed his mind and chased them with his army. Moses and the Israelites were surrounded by mountains (circumstances), a wilderness (missteps), the pharaoh (regression), and the Red Sea (the answer) in front of them.

If Moses didn't understand the ways of God, He would have assumed, like some did, that God brought them there to die. That would have been a big misunderstanding! However, Moses didn't run in fear. He was patient enough to wait for the Red Sea to open.

He knew without a shadow of a doubt that the Lord was going to deliver them. Not only did the Lord open up the Red Sea for them, but He also closed it on their enemies.

I'm sure the children of Israel were wondering, as I often have, "God, how come you can't just deliver me without all the drama?" However, God's way is mature. Allow yourself to grow in Him. Grow in the Word and the gifts and talents He has given you. And don't be hung up by mistakes. They're part of the learning process. Just repent, adjust, and correct when you fall short.

You don't get angry at a toddler who's learning how to walk when he stumbles and falls. "I can't believe you fell" doesn't sound right because the toddler is learning. Determination causes the toddler to get back up and, without interference, he walks again until it's natural. Had his parents not let him stumble and fall and get back up on his own, that child's trip to the Olympics could've been stifled by a lack of independence. God likens us to this toddler. He awaits the day we follow His lead consistently, so He doesn't have to intervene.

God's way confounds the enemy (1 Corinthians 1:27). It was the Lord who instructed Moses and the people to camp by the sea, fully surrounded.

He wanted their enemy, Pharaoh, to think they were confused. Even when you don't see a way of escape, trust what God has said to you, and decide to walk it all the way out. Don't misunderstand what's taking place; the confusion is for the enemy. God's way is safe. He has prepared it through His love.

God's way is also peaceful. Have you ever experienced natural safety without peace of mind? Or unexplainable peace in the midst of natural insecurity? Those misunderstandings can cause big disturbances if left unchecked. The Word reminds us there's nothing new under the sun, and with every temptation, the Lord makes a way of escape.

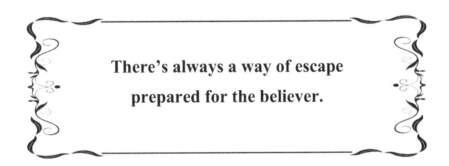

There's always a way of escape prepared for the believer.

If there is none present in plain sight, expect one to be created. Are you willing to wait long enough for your Red Sea to open? (1 Corinthians 10:13).

God is always mindful of us (every part: mind, spirit, body) and simply asks us to hold our peace, so we can enjoy freedom from disturbance. Nothing should disturb what God has said to you no matter what it looks like.

God's way grants authority. Spending some time with God and His word will help you know His thoughts. When you begin to say what He tells you to say, you'll feel no shame because you will have already spent time with Him and understand how He does things. He increases your authority in your time with Him. Learn to be comfortable taking dominion and being in charge. It's God's way and your right.

Moses understood his rights. He knew God equipped him with hands full of answers (the rod). He knew he could hear God, who said, "Lift up your rod and stretch out your hand." But most importantly, Moses understood the Lord had already equipped him to overcome every situation he'd face in his lifetime. When you read Exodus, notice that, throughout that process, Moses responded with "He will deliver us" because he understood how God worked. And God will deliver you too!

God desires to make you whole, not just provide immediate relief. There goes that "above and abundantly" God we know. His reputation is irrefutable. When you ask God, He gives His Word, and through His Word He reveals His ways to you. Along with His ways, He gives you wisdom to accomplish a task. If you don't follow His ways, you'll misunderstand Him every time. So consult Him. He loves you so much. The Lord loves you past what anyone knows about you. You know that part of your life you really haven't shared with anyone? We all have a part. He knows that part of you, but if you believe Him past what you think you deserve, He will still bless you and give you the desires of your heart.

I pray there will be no misunderstandings between you and God. I declare that every lie and deception that has been presented to you is exposed and you experience the true love that God has for you, as His own. Amen.

NOTES

Chapter 10

DESIRE AND DELIGHT

WE KNOW GOD WILL GIVE US THE DESIRES OF OUR hearts when we delight ourselves in Him (Psalm 37:4). This means He will give to you beyond your wants. Giving you the desires of your heart is like placing a letter in your hand. The Lord does the same thing with a desire, except He puts it in your heart. This desire may be for you and an answer for others. All of heaven is backing you when you agree with the desire He has placed in your heart.

When you delight yourself in Him, no matter where you are in life, you allow yourself to be happy and satisfied with being with Him. You may have desires that haven't come to pass because you're not satisfied with Him. If you're still looking for people or things to make you happy, you're not delighting yourself in God. It's a great possibility that your desires are outside of Him. Your plans may not include Him at all. You'll know which ones exclude Him when you consult with Him.

I had a conversation with a young lady one day, and she told me she was believing God to purchase a new house to bless someone else. She had desired to do so for some time, so I asked her, "Did you ask God for instructions?" She explained she hadn't thought of that. "I thought asking for the money to buy the house was enough." Well, it's not.

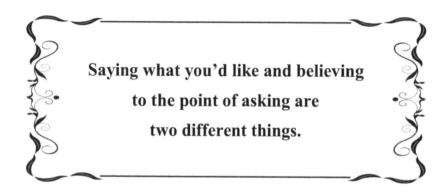

Saying what you'd like and believing to the point of asking are two different things.

If you believe the Lord gave you the desire to buy someone a house, ask Him some questions. Do you want me to buy it now? How do you want me to obtain this home? What area is it in, and what does it look like?

Her prayer should have sounded something like this. "God I believe you are my source, and when You want me to purchase this property, I'll be sensitive to hear you say this is the one to buy. I thank you for showing me the house, and I thank you for giving me the favor and the ability to obtain it. In Jesus's name, Amen."

Now, let us stop here for a moment because I'm speaking from the perspective of faith being alive. There has to be some action on your part, or your faith in this area is dead. Remember the scripture that tells us faith without works is dead (James 2:26)? I'm sure the young lady didn't have all the money, the credit, or the self-ability to purchase the house at the time, but she had a willing heart. However, focusing on her situation in the moment was stopping her from fulfilling the desire God placed in her heart. She might have thought, "I don't have the money or the credit. I own my own home, but my house isn't paid off, and I need to make sure I'm debt-free to do this. When all these things are taken care of, and I have financial abundance, I can purchase this home for this other person."

That's not faith alive. God had no room in the young lady's process to work a miracle because she was working under her own ingenuity. God doesn't need her money, her credit, or for all her bills to be paid off to accomplish this act through her. Who said He wanted her to purchase the home? Maybe God wanted her to be sensitive enough to be in the right place at the right time and receive the home.

God doesn't think the way we think, remember? But He will give us His thoughts on a matter if we ask. He may want her to take a house gifted to her and give it away as a seed. The Bible says he provides seed to the sower (2 Corinthians 9:10). Everything given to you isn't yours to keep. At times, God supplies it to you as a seed for something bigger. A house gifted to her could be a seed for the business empire she is believing for. But the harvest will never come until the seed is sown. She has what it takes, which is a willing heart.

God doesn't need your money when He decides to do something. He is your source. The only thing preventing or delaying your desire is that you need to mix it with faith. Once you hear the Lord say something, you have to use your faith and go after it by seeking Him for instructions on how to get it done.

When I had to go out of town for a speaking engagement, I told the Lord how much I disliked speaking. In truth, I was in fear of succeeding and the criticism it brings. I didn't mind ministering to others, but I preferred to do it one on one. In addition, I didn't feel comfortable negotiating the cost for travel, hotel rooms, transportation, and food.

All these necessities must be accommodated for, but the conversation made me uncomfortable. Because of this, I sometimes declined opportunities to speak.

One day, the Lord told me, *I am about to open some opportunities for you, and it will require some traveling. Therefore, do not turn down any speaking engagements during this period.* I hadn't realize, by saying "I don't want to do this," in the past, I was rejecting the desire he was trying to put in my heart regarding speaking engagements. I felt I had been obedient in most cases by sacrificing and going regardless of how I felt, but the Word of God tells us in order to eat the good of the land, we have to be willing and obedient, not just obedient. (Isaiah 1:19) Therefore, I had to repent to the Lord for not being willing to go.

As soon as I said yes, doors began to open. I told the Lord, "Look. I work for You. Therefore, all my needs I'm giving to you, and for this event coming up, here is the amount I desire." I got exactly what I asked for. I was amazed at the accuracy to the penny.

While sitting there in awe of what the Lord had done, I heard Him whisper peacefully within me, *Ask me again.* I knew what that meant, and I couldn't stop the tears from flowing.

I know for sure He'd heard me, and God was asking me to prove Him again. In Malachi 3, the Lord says, "Prove me now." When He says this, He wants to show you, *when you trust in what I say by being obedient to My instructions, I will demonstrate my word to you.* He wants you to have repeated victories when you practice biblical principles. I had stepped into a side of God that He wanted me to get familiar with. He doesn't just meet needs; He cares about us and what we desire.

I took a deep breath, and I asked again, but this time I asked for more. "Lord, when I come back to this state to speak again, I would like double." Then, I got bold and decided to practice some more by taking it a step further and said, "Lord before I leave town tomorrow, I want to go on a shopping spree, and I don't want to spend any money." I gave Him praise, and I got dressed.

I had a lunch appointment with the host who had invited me as a speaker. Her plan was to show me around town and make a stop at one of their beautiful beaches. However, there were so many interruptions, we enjoyed, that we only had time for lunch. As we left the restaurant, she realized it was too late to go to the beach, so she turned off into a shopping center.

The next thing I knew, we were shopping. As I entered the store, I heard the Lord say, *Choose whatever you want from these four racks.* So I carefully went through the racks and got everything I wanted. I mean everything. Now, because all our items were in the same cart, I removed mine once we were at the checkout. I would never take advantage of someone and assume they're paying my bill even though my request to the Lord was for a paid for shopping spree.

Once the cashier completed the host's transaction, the host told her, "Please give us separate bags, but put everything on one bill. I'll also be paying for her merchandise." My mind was blown. God not only heard me, but He also wanted me to try Him. He wanted me to experience more of Him.

As if that weren't enough, as we left the store, she turned to me, put money in my hand, and said, "This is for you. I told the Lord I had a desire to take you shopping and bless you." I wondered if it was really her desire or if God had put that desire in her heart because I'd asked for it earlier. Either way, I am amazed. God gave me above what I asked Him for that morning. He gave me the desires of my heart. Imagine if I'd been too afraid to ask!

Having a desire doesn't mean the idea originated with you. Remember He sometimes puts the desire there. Normally, those desires are good ideas that keep coming to your mind to help others, but deep down inside, you tell yourself you don't really want to do that. Yet, it keeps coming up. Spend some time with God and ask Him, "Is this a desire you're trying to give me?"

Don't be afraid to ask God. He wants you to ask Him. Life experiences and disappointments can keep us from asking because we don't want to be hurt and confused again. We think if we don't ask, we won't expect, and if we don't expect, we won't hope and believe, building ourselves up for a big letdown. This happens when we fail to understand the ways of God because of the way we think.

Before I agreed to obey God, I had the goods to speak to audiences, but I was too terrified to use them. I enjoyed talking to people, but I was afraid of the crowds, so I didn't want to make speaking engagements a regular part of my life.

I was so stuck on not getting anything wrong when it came to helping people that I didn't allow myself to get anything right. God isn't looking for perfection. He's looking for a willingness of heart.

He's looking for someone who will keep going, regardless of what happens, because you believe Him.

You can do this! You know the full process of A.S.K.! You have an understanding of God's ways, and when you don't understand, you know how to consult Him and ask for directions. You know how to take those instructions He has given you and mix them with faith.

Forget about your experiences. Forget about what people have said and done in the past. Forget statistics and time wasted. God can redeem your time.

I can hear the Lord saying, *I'm not asking you to make it happen. It's My job to perform My word. Just believe again. Trust Me and believe.*

I pray on today that your way of thinking has been changed and His ways are constantly being revealed to you. I pray that what you have learned will cause you to come into agreement with God, without doubt, causing Him to perform His word quickly. Amen.

When you are taking those steps towards asking, know your God is there to guide you. Go ahead, believe all things are possible, and A.S.K.!

NOTES

Acknowledgments

I thank God for all He has done for me. Loving me unconditionally. Having patience with me until I was willing to put myself in a place to understand His Word and grow. I thank Him for not giving up on me all the times I blamed Him for what I was going through, not knowing I was choosing to live beneath my privilege. I thank Him for how my life turned out.

I had no idea how much I'd misunderstood. I didn't fully comprehend His Word and His ways, but He never gave up on me, and I am so thankful. When I decided to take Him at His Word, His Word came alive in my life. It jumped off the pages and became a reality.

He even came in and redeemed the time I'd wasted feeling sorry for myself. He put me in the place where I would have been if I had start believing Him ten years earlier. He's more than life to me.

I thank Him for changing my heart and mind, so I can believe on Him as Scripture has said. Because of that, out of my belly flow rivers of living water. I've seen things I wanted for years finally come to pass over months.

I thank Him for every single life experience because I believed Him when He said all things, good and bad, work together. I cannot have one without the other, but they work together and become good for me. I thank Him for sending people into my life who were good for me and wanted success for me as much as I did. They showed His love for me with patience when fear paralyzed me and kept me from moving forward.

My life is not the same, and I cannot thank God enough for His love for me, the process, and the people with whom He has blessed me. They were truly God sent.

Dr. Stacie Kelley, my friend who asked of the Lord. It was you He answered that day. Thank you for your friendship, transparency, insight, and encouragement.

Aisja (Angel) Robinson, my help during the writing of this book. You nudged me on all the way, every Tuesday afternoon at 2:00. Thank you for designing the book cover and your assistance with the book marker. You are amazing!

Candice Embrey, who became my editor before the editor, you stuck by my side and worked to keep me in order even when you did not fully understand. I thank God for you.

QB, OB, and CBx5, (Dynamic 7) thank you all for the encouraging words and the sacrifices you've made with understanding. Wow! I could not have asked for a better FamBam!

To my son, CB3, Christian, you came right on time, tied up loose ends, and helped with my photos and the book cover. Thank you for all you do. I am so proud of you.

And of course, I saved the best for last. Pastor Owen Black, you are my love and my best friend. You have been my true supporter in things possible and those things that appeared to be impossible. You are always present and a present from God. Thank you for loving me unconditionally, believing in the God in me, and allowing me to move as He directs. No man can put a price on that. I love you!

Love to you all,
Audrey A. Black

AUDREY BLACK MINISTRIES
PRESENTS...

THE JOURNAL

BONUS MATERIAL AVAILABLE

www.audreyblack.org

Free Journal
(for limited time only)
To help you continue your
new prayer journey

ASK

SEEK

KNOCK

Bookmarker

Written by Audrey Black
while supplies last

at

www.audreyblack.org

Beyond
the hustle and the bustle

The traffic and all the loud,

You can rise beyond the worry

And be
above the clouds.

There is so much space and territory

That no
one has yet taken,

Move into miracles and wonders

The
space is yet still vacant.

Although you can view it in a plane

To get
there is not the same,

And
there's a promise for the people

That
yet still remains.

Some believers have come close

But
their Faith did not last.

Not knowing in order to get there

All
they needed to do was

A.S.K.

CPSIA information can be obtained
at www.ICGtesting.com
Printed in the USA
BVHW070928310123
657444BV00004B/183